Pablo PICASSO

Pablo
PICASSO

Gareth Stevens Publishing
A WORLD ALMANAC EDUCATION GROUP COMPANY

Please visit our web site at:
www.worldalmanaclibrary.com
For a free color catalog describing World Almanac®
Library's list of high-quality books and multimedia
programs, call 1-800-848-2928 (USA) or 1-800-387-3178
(Canada). World Almanac® Library's fax: (414) 332-3567.

Library of Congress Cataloging-in-Publication Data available upon request
from publisher. Fax (414) 336-0157 for the attention of the Publishing
Records Department.

ISBN 0-8368-5601-5 (lib. bdg.)
ISBN 0-8368-5606-6 (softcover)

This North American edition first published in 2004 by
World Almanac® Library
330 West Olive Street, Suite 100
Milwaukee, WI 53212 USA

This U.S. edition copyright © 2004 by World Almanac® Library.
Original edition copyright © 2004 McRae Books Srl.

The series "The Lives of the Artists"
was created and produced by McRae Books Srl
Borgo Santa Croce, 8 – Florence (Italy)
info@mcraebooks.com
Publishers: Anne McRae and Marco Nardi

Project Editor: Loredana Agosta
Art History consultant: Roberto Carvalho de Magalhães
Text: Susie Hodge
Illustrations: Studio Stalio (Alessandro Cantucci,
Fabiano Fabbrucci, Andrea Morandi)
Graphic Design: Marco Nardi
Picture Research: Loredana Agosta
Layout: Studio Yotto
World Almanac® Library editor: JoAnn Early Macken
World Almanac® Library art direction: Tammy Gruenewald

Acknowledgments
All efforts have been made to obtain and provide compensation for
the copyright to the photos and artworks in this book in accordance
with legal provisions. Persons who may nevertheless still have claims
are requested to contact the copyright owners. All works by Pablo
Picasso: ©2003 The Estate of Pablo Picasso by SIAE, Rome

t=top; tl=top left; tc=top center; tr=top right; c=center; cl=center left; cr=
center right; b=bottom; bl=bottom left; bc=bottom center; br=bottom
right

The publishers would like to thank the following archives who have
authorized the reproduction of the works in this book:
The Bridgeman Art Library, London/Farabola Foto, Milano: 6, 9b, 10, 11t,
12b, 14bl, 16cl, 20, 21bl, 25tr, 27b, 29tr, 29cr, 34–35, 35tr, 37bl, 42c, 43t, 43cl,
43b; Foto Scala, Florence: cover, 9, 13br, 21br, 22br, 23c, 24bl, 30b, 42bl,
44bl; ©Photo RMN: P.Gérin/TEI-D.Chareyron 4, 40b, 41b, J.G. Berizzi 5,
27t, Béatrice Hatala 18l, 28t, 30c, 37br, 44t, R.G. Ojeda 28b, 31t, Franck
Raux 31b, 38t, Daniel Arnaudet 41cl; ©CNAC/MNAM/Dist RMN:
Christian Bahier and Philippe Migeat 24–25; Corbis/Contrasto, Milan:
Archivio Iconografico, S.A. 11b, Hulton-Deutsch Collection 12cl, Francis
G. Mayer 13cr, 14br, 17, Edimédia 15tr, Burstein Collection 15c,
Philadelphia Musuem of Art 16cr, Bettmann 32c; Rue des Archives,
Paris: 8br, 15b, 23t, 29cl, 39tr, 40c, 45cr; Photos12, Paris/Grazia Neri, Srl,
Milan: 36t, 36b, 37t, 39tl, 41tr; Lonely Planet Images: Neil Setchfield 7t,
Tom Levy 45tr; The Image Works 7c

The publishers would like to thank the following museums and
institutions who have authorized the reproduction of the works in this
book: Digital Image © 2003 The Museum of Modern Art/Scala,
Florence: 18–19, 21tl, 22tl, 26b, 30tr, 39b; ©Tate, London 2003: 3, 33;
Museu Picasso ©Photo Arxiu Fotografic de Museus, Ajuntament de
Barcelona: 8c; ©Succession H. Matisse by SIAE 2003: 17; The Art
Institute of Chicago: 26t; The Minneapolis Institute of Arts: 21tl

Printed in China

1 2 3 4 5 6 7 8 9 08 07 06 05 04

cover: *The Dream*, Ganz Collection, New York

above: *War*, Temple de la Paix, Vallauris

opposite: *The Pipes of Pan* (detail), Musée Picasso, Paris

previous page: *Weeping Woman*, Tate Gallery, London

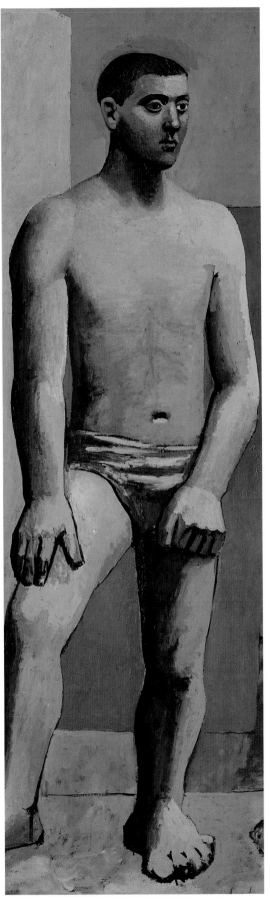

Table of Contents

Introduction

Pablo Picasso was arguably the most famous artist of the twentieth century. During his career, which lasted more than seventy-five years, he produced thousands of works, including drawings, paintings, sculpture, prints, and ceramics. He changed his style more often and more profoundly than any other artist, and he can be credited with almost single-handedly creating modern art. Working with incredible speed and vitality, he took inspiration from many different sources, constantly inventing new ways of creating art, even if they went against everyone else's methods. Although he was born in Spain, he spent most of his adult life in France.

▶ *An advertising pole in Paris showing some of the exciting events that attracted Picasso there.*

▲ *In 1907, Picasso painted this* Self-Portrait *with masklike features, flat colors, and black lines, surprising the art world with his radical and innovative style.*

A Modern Artistic Genius

Widely considered to be the most influential artist of his time, Picasso inspired many artistic styles. In the first decades of the twentieth century, he and the artist Georges Braque (1882–1963) invented a new pictorial language called Cubism, inspiring many artists and motivating many other art movements, such as Futurism, Neoplasticism, and abstract painting. His use of unexpected materials in his collages and constructions also became a significant part of twentieth-century art.

Picasso's SPAIN

La Coruña · Barcelona

· Madrid

· Malaga

▲ *The Guggenheim Museum in New York is just one of the museums and art galleries throughout the world where Picasso's works are displayed.*

A Legend

Even during Picasso's lifetime, many exhibitions were dedicated to his work. He was a popular yet controversial character, and he became extremely wealthy. His desire to create new forms and to give an original vision of the world never ceased, and he worked until the day he died. Fully aware of his talents, he once said, "I wanted to be a painter and I became Picasso."

In Picasso's Time

The world changed enormously during Picasso's lifetime. He lived through two world wars and experienced some of the greatest advances in technology, such as the invention of cars, radios, and airplanes and the use of electricity and telephones.

▶ *When Picasso was growing up, electric lights were only just beginning to light the cities of Europe and the United States. The word "electric" came to stand for "modern."*

▶ *A twentieth-century poster for a French political party. After World War II, Picasso faced harsh criticism because he became a member of the Communist party.*

An Artist of Many Talents

Picasso's talents lay in all aspects of art. He created over twenty thousand works and experimented with many mediums, producing works in paint, bronze, ceramics, print, and more. He always seemed to be one step ahead of everyone else, changing his use of materials and style with incredible ease and invention. Every time he changed his style, he seemed also to change parts of his life — wives, lovers, children, homes, and friends.

◀ *Woman's Head (1931) is on display in the Musée Picasso in Paris, along with over 3,500 engravings, paintings, ceramic works, and drawings, many donated by Picasso's family and friends.*

▼ *One of Picasso's most famous works,* Guernica *(1937), showing the horrors of war, is in the Museo Nacional Reina Sofia in Madrid.*

Where to Find Picasso

Picasso's work, from his juvenile drawings to his huge canvases, has received an enormous amount of attention. Because he was so famous, even during his lifetime, entire museums were dedicated to him. Two of the most famous are the Museu Picasso in Barcelona and the Musée Picasso in Paris. Picasso's work can also be found in many other museums worldwide. Huge sums of money have been paid for his work because no modern art collection seems complete without at least one Picasso.

Young Picasso

1881 Pablo Diego José Francisco de Paula Juan Nepomuceno María de los Remedios Crispriano de la Santísima Trinidad (Picasso) is born in Málaga, Spain.
1884 Picasso's sister Dolores, known as Lola, is born.
1887 His sister Concepcíon, known as Conchita, is born.
1891 The family moves to northwest Spain, where Picasso's father, Don José, begins working at Da Guarda Art School.
1892 Picasso enters Da Guarda Art School.
1895 Conchita dies of diphtheria. The family moves to Barcelona, where Don José becomes professor of La Llotja Academy of Art. Picasso enters La Llotja and meets Manuel Pallarès. He paints his first major oil painting, *First Communion*.
1896 He has his first studio in Barcelona with Pallarès. *First Communion* is exhibited in Barcelona.

In 1880, Don José Ruiz Blasco, a painter, museum curator, and art teacher from a respected family in Málaga, in southern Spain, married Doña María Picasso y López, also from Málaga. The following year, the first of their three children, Pablo, was born. Picasso, as he would later be called, showed talent at an early age. According to legend, when Pablo was still a boy, his father handed him his own paintbrushes, saying that Pablo was a far better artist than his father was.

▲ *Barcelona has always attracted inventive architects such as Antonio Gaudí, whose cathedral, the Sagrada Familia, begun in the 1880s, towers over the city like a huge sculpture.*

Barcelona

Barcelona, located in the Catalonia region of Spain, is not far from the Mediterranean Sea. It is full of magnificent buildings and bustling streets and has long been known as a welcoming city for artists, writers, and designers. When Picasso's family moved there in 1895, it was a modern industrial town with a rapidly growing population. Its textile industry helped Catalonia become one of the wealthiest regions in Spain.

▲ Bullfight *and* Doves *(1892). Picasso was a child prodigy in art. These are some early drawings he made.*

The Making of an Artist
Picasso's first word was "Piz!" — short for *lápiz*, meaning pencil in Spanish. His father encouraged him to draw and took him to bullfights. When he was nine years old, he made his first painting, of a bullfight. The following year, the family moved to La Coruña on the Atlantic coast. Picasso continued showing outstanding talent, and Don José let him complete some of his own paintings.

▶ *Picasso in 1885 at age four.*

The Prado

When Picasso was fourteen, the family visited the Prado, Spain's national art museum in Madrid. There he saw works by some of the greatest masters of the Spanish school, including Diego Velázquez (1599–1660), El Greco (1541–1614), and Francisco de Goya (1746–1828).

▼ *Along with other art students, Picasso was taught to draw classical sculpture like this copy of a Roman statue.*

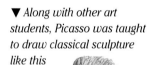

▲ The Third of May *(1808) by Goya presents a shocking picture of Spanish citizens being shot at close range by French soldiers. It commemorated a real event that happened in 1808.*

Picasso's Training

The professors at La Llotja Academy, where Picasso studied, were astonished: in a day, he completed exercises that took older students over a month to do! Picasso was taught in the classical tradition, studying masterpieces of the past, particularly ancient Greek and Roman sculpture.

Art Before Picasso

Art was expected to follow rules that had been handed down for centuries, but by the time Picasso was born, some artists, such as the Impressionists and the Postimpressionists, were challenging these traditions. A new decorative style, Art Nouveau, was flourishing worldwide.

▶ The Kitchen Table *(1888–90) by Paul Cézanne (1839–1906). Cézanne was a revolutionary who questioned artistic traditions.*

Early Works

Picasso began his career in the bohemian circles of Barcelona, where the poets, painters, musicians, and intellectuals of the day spent their time in lively and heated discussion at cafés. During this time, Picasso formed friendships that later had a profound effect on both his life and artistic career. Then in 1900, just before his nineteenth birthday, he traveled with his friend and fellow painter Carlos Casagemas to the center of the modern art world — Paris.

1897 In a café in Barcelona, Els Quatre Gats, Picasso paints portraits, which are displayed on the walls. He begins studying at Madrid's Royal Academy of San Fernando, but he leaves within months.

1898 He falls ill and stays in Horta de San Juan with Pallarés. He wins medals in Madrid and Málaga.

1899 He returns to Barcelona and works as a painter and illustrator for magazines. He meets painters Joan Miró (1893–1983) and Carlos Casagemas and writer Jaime Sabartés. Works on his first etching, *El Picador*.

1900 His first exhibition is held at Els Quatre Gats. He and Casagemas go to Paris. Art dealer Pedro Mañach offers him 150 francs a month in exchange for some works and becomes his first dealer. Returns to Spain and settles in Madrid the next year.

▶ Le Moulin de la Galette *(1900), Picasso's first Paris painting, shows his interest in the work of the Impressionists and Toulouse-Lautrec.*

◀ *For the 1889 International Exposition, engineer Gustave Eiffel (1832–1923) built a tall iron tower to demonstrate the progress of French engineering. At first, many Parisians complained that it spoiled the city, but it soon became a symbol of Paris.*

▲ *Visitors traveled to see the amazing International Exposition. They sent postcards like this to their families and friends at home.*

Painting in Paris

In 1900, Picasso and his friend Casagemas went to the International Exposition in Paris. They saw works by the Impressionists there and in private galleries. For two months, the young artists rented a studio in Paris. Picasso worked and sold some of his paintings.

1900s

The International Exposition, or World's Fair, in Paris was a dazzling display of achievement marking the dawn of the twentieth century. Millions of visitors arrived from all over the world to see exhibits showing how the world was changing as industry and new technology transformed the way people lived and worked. Picasso's painting *Les Dernier Moments* was selected to be displayed in the section on Spanish art.

The Four Cats

In 1897, Picasso began going to a new café in Barcelona, Els Quatre Gats — the Four Cats, where forward-thinking artists and writers met. In the café's artistic circle, he met other painters who introduced him to the works of the French artist Henri de Toulouse-Lautrec (1864–1901). Picasso also exhibited his work and painted the portraits of the local artists at the café.

▶ En el Moulin Rouge: el baile *(1890) by Toulouse-Lautrec. His work made a powerful impression on Picasso. His posters and paintings made use of clear colors and flowing lines.*

First Major Works

In 1897, Picasso painted his second major oil painting, *Science and Charity*, which was praised at the Fine Arts General Exhibition in Madrid and won a gold medal in Málaga. His father used his contacts with newspaper critics to influence how the press received the painting. Don José was an extremely powerful presence in his son's early life, but Picasso broke away as he grew up.

▼ Science and Charity *(1897). Picasso produced this work at the age of fifteen. His father posed as the doctor.*

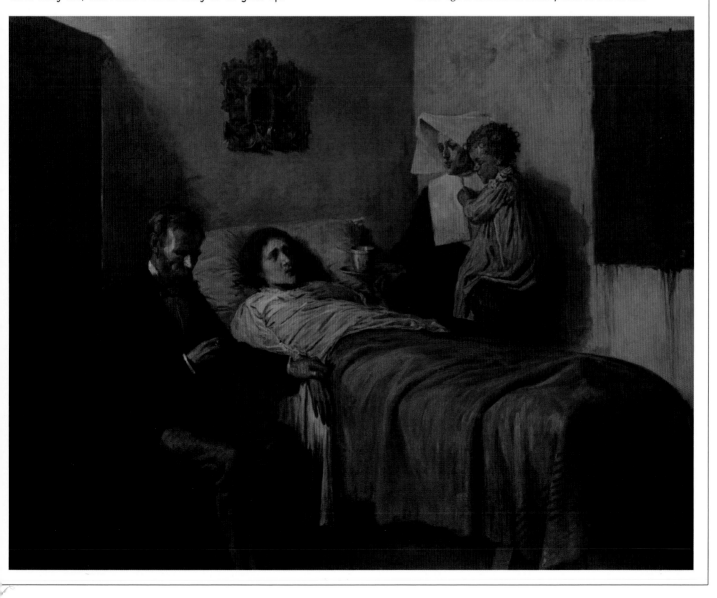

The Blue Period

1901 Casagemas commits suicide. Picasso begins to paint blue pictures. He goes to Madrid to work for *Arte Joven* magazine. When the magazine folds, he returns to Paris and moves into Casagemas' former studio. He meets the writer Max Jacob, and his first Paris show is well reviewed.
1902 After his contract with art dealer Pedro Mañach is broken, Picasso returns to Barcelona. In October, he returns to Paris for the third time but has money problems. He lives with Jacob and exhibits pictures from his Blue Period in a group show in Paris.
1903 He returns to Barcelona and produces over fifty paintings.
c. 1903 He produces some small sculptural works.

From 1900, Picasso made eight trips back and forth between Spain and Paris, finally settling in Paris in 1904. He had terrible money problems. In 1901, he started signing his pictures "Picasso" to show his independence from his father. In February of the same year, his friend Casagemas committed suicide. Over the next four years — his so-called Blue Period — the color blue dominated many of Picasso's pictures, showing his anguish.

▲ *By 1901, Picasso believed that his father tried to dominate him too much, so he began signing all his work with the single name Picasso, after his mother.*

Max Jacob

▶ *After early money problems, Jacob wrote many successful novels and poems. He died in a concentration camp in World War II.*

Max Jacob (1876–1944) was an impoverished writer whose work influenced many artists. On Picasso's third visit to Paris, he shared a studio with Jacob, and their friendship helped strengthen Picasso's position in the Paris art community. Because they were both so poor, however, life was miserable. Picasso worked all night while Jacob slept in their only bed. During the day, Jacob worked while Picasso slept.

Carlos Casagemas

Picasso had met Carlos Casagemas at Els Quatre Gats in Barcelona. When they went to Paris together in October of 1900, they settled in a little studio in Montmartre, a run-down area where many artists lived. That same year, Picasso went home to Spain for Christmas so that Casagemas could recover from a broken love affair. While Picasso was in Madrid, Casagemas shot himself in a café. After Picasso returned to Paris in 1901, his Blue Period began.

▶ Evocation (The Burial of Casagemas) *(1901) was the first painting of Picasso's Blue Period. Friends and family gather around Casagemas' body. Above, Casagemas rides a white horse toward heaven. Picasso said, "I began to paint in blue when I realized that Casagemas had died."*

▼ *This detail of a sixteenth-century painting by El Greco shows how he lengthened his figures to show their saintliness.*

Blue El Grecos

During his Blue Period, Picasso stretched and elongated the proportions of his figures like those of El Greco, whose work had fascinated him since he first saw it in the Prado Museum in Madrid. By changing his style, Picasso was showing his independence and originality as an artist. Like Vincent van Gogh (1853–90), Paul Gauguin (1848–1903), and others before him, Picasso assumed that the appearance of the figures as they are in reality is less important than the ideas and feelings they express. Compare these figures with those of *Science and Charity* (page 11).

▼ Poor People on the Seashore *(1903) shows a cold, hungry family, each figure elongated in the style of El Greco.*

Sad Subjects

Like the Dutch artist van Gogh, whose work he had seen in Paris, Picasso used color to show human misery and sadness. Color was used to show people's feelings rather than to render only their appearance. Picasso chose the color blue to express despair and anguish in his works.

▼ The Absinthe Drinker *(1901) is typical of Picasso's Blue Period. Everything seems desolate — the glass, the bottle, and the woman, with her long fingers and angular face, hugging herself.*

The Rose Period

1904 Picasso settles in a studio in Montmartre. He meets Fernande Olivier (1881–1966), Guillaume Apollinaire, and other writers and artists. He begins visiting the circus.
1905 In a group show in Paris, Picasso exhibits his first Rose Period works. Leo and Gertrude Stein begin to buy his paintings. Visits Schoorl, Holland, in the summer and paints young Dutch women.
1906 Art dealer Ambroise Vollard buys many paintings.

Settling in Paris, Picasso became a part of a circle of writers, actors, musicians, and artists and met and fell in love with his first model, Fernande Olivier. During this time, his palette changed. His blue tones were replaced with pinks, creams, oranges, soft greens, blues, and yellows, marking the beginning of his Rose Period. He painted scenes of circus life and created his first sculptures. New contacts with art dealers and collectors also made life a bit more rosy.

Life in Montmartre

Picasso still lived in Montmartre among all the other artists and writers. His friend Jacob nicknamed his rented studio the "Bateau-Lavoir," or wash boat, because of its shape and dampness. Picasso often met his friends at a bar called Le Lapin Agile — the agile rabbit, where the landlord accepted paintings as payment instead of money.

Summer in Gósol

In May of 1906, Picasso and Fernande, his new love, traveled to Gósol, a tiny Spanish village in the Pyrenees. The works he produced there show a return to classical themes with a style inspired by ancient Greek art.

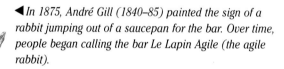

◀ *In 1875, André Gill (1840–85) painted the sign of a rabbit jumping out of a saucepan for the bar. Over time, people began calling the bar Le Lapin Agile (the agile rabbit).*

U.S. Patrons

On his return to Paris, Picasso began selling more of his work, particularly to the U.S. collectors Leo and Gertrude Stein. Leo (1872–1947) was an accomplished art critic, and his sister Gertrude (1874–1946) was a writer who drew many writers and artists into her circle. All three became good friends, particularly Picasso and Gertrude. During the winter of 1905–6, Picasso painted her portrait.

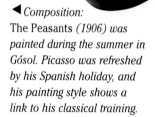

◀*Composition: The Peasants (1906) was painted during the summer in Gósol. Picasso was refreshed by his Spanish holiday, and his painting style shows a link to his classical training.*

▶ *The Portrait of Gertrude Stein (1906) was painted fairly realistically at first. Just before Picasso finished it, he repainted the face with flat color and masklike features. It marked the beginning of a dramatic change in his art.*

The Circus

Picasso frequently visited the nearby Circus Médrano. For about six months, he painted the circus folk — clowns, tightrope walkers, and troupes of acrobats called saltimbanques. Saltimbanques were wandering acrobats who performed in various circuses. Picasso was interested in the way show people create different personalities when dressed in their costumes, often hiding their real feelings. He identified with Harlequin, the unsmiling clown, and portrayed him as someone who amused people even if he felt sad underneath.

▶ *In* Mother and Child *(1905), two acrobats have just come home after a performance. The mother and son are cuddling close, tired and almost as sad as the figures from the Blue Period.*

◀ *In 1906, Picasso created this bronze sculpture,* Head of a Woman (Fernande), *inspired by his new love and model.*

▼ *Apollinaire's work was often concerned with the clash between modern and traditional creative ideas.*

Guillaume Apollinaire

Guillaume Apollinaire (1880–1918) was a poet, writer, and art critic who became one of Picasso's good friends. They lived near each other in Montmartre and often met at Le Lapin Agile. At the start of the twentieth century, Apollinaire was an important part of several avant-garde movements in French literature and art. He was also friends with the artists Maurice de Vlaminick (1876–1958) and André Derain (1880–1954). He introduced the artists of his day to African sculpture and to the work of Henri Rousseau (1844–1910).

A New Style

1906 In the Louvre Museum in Paris, Picasso sees an exhibition of Iberian sculpture. Gertrude Stein introduces him to Henri Matisse and André Derain. Art dealer Vollard buys most of his Rose Period works, solving Picasso's financial problems. **1907** He paints *Self-Portrait* in a new style (see page 6) and buys two Iberian stone heads. *Les Demoiselles d'Avignon* shocks his fellow artists. Kahnweiler becomes his dealer. He is introduced to Georges Braque.

From the winter of 1905, Picasso kept experimenting with new ideas. When he returned from Spain with Fernande, he changed his style again. This was first noticed in the *Portrait of Gertrude Stein*. Many people complained that the portrait was too masklike, but from this time, Picasso laid the foundations of modern art. His painting *Les Demoiselles d'Avignon* not only marked an important change in his personal career but set a new course for the development of modern art as well.

New Sources of Inspiration

Both Picasso's painting in Gósol and his experiments with sculpture had given him ideas. Impressed by the uncomplicated shapes and exaggerated features of ancient Iberian sculpture, Picasso began to simplify the way he painted human figures and faces.

Cézanne's Legacy

Cézanne, one of the greatest artists of the day, emphasized the geometric structure of his subjects. He believed that "everything in nature is modeled on the sphere, the cylinder, and the cone." In 1907, a year after his death, a large and popular exhibition of his work was held in Paris. The abstract quality of some of his late works inspired Picasso.

▲ The Large Bathers *(1906) is one of Cézanne's last paintings. Although the figures look unfinished and sketchy, he took great care over them, painting them from several different angles at once.*

▶ *Because everyone knew that Picasso could paint realistically,* Self-Portrait with Palette *(1906) shows that he was purposefully changing his style.*

The Fauves

In 1905, a small group of artists shocked critics in Paris with wild, vibrant paintings. Henri Matisse (1869–1954) had joined with André Derain, Maurice de Vlaminck, and Albert Marquet (1875–1947) to show some vividly colorful works at the annual exhibition of new art, the Salon d'Automne. Critics and the public thought that the work was too bright, unrealistic, and childlike, and one critic said it was like being surrounded by *fauves* (meaning "wild beasts"). Today, Fauvism is recognized as the first avant-garde art movement, and Matisse is seen as one of the most important influences on modern art.

▶ Open Window, Collioure *(1905) was one of Matisse's paintings that he showed at the Salon d'Automne. He painted in a fresh way, using bold colors and brush strokes.*

Henri-Matisse

A New Style

▼ *Picasso's* Tête de personnage *(1907) is an example of a wooden sculpture carved in his new style.*

Shocking Beauty

During 1906–7, Picasso made many sketches for his painting *Les Demoiselles d'Avignon*. When Picasso unveiled the finished painting, even his most modern-thinking friends were shocked at what Picasso had done to the classical subject of a group of female nudes. "It's a hoax!" cried Matisse, horrified. Then they realized that Picasso had invented a new language for art using a combination of ideas from all over the world, abandoning traditional ideas of painting just for beauty.

▶ Les Demoiselles d'Avignon *(1907) is often called the most important painting of the twentieth century. The angular human figures look like wooden sculpture, their faces a mixture of Iberian and African masks. The fruit is a reference to Cézanne. Old and new images blend to create a revolution in art.*

Sculpture

In Gósol and at the Louvre Museum, Picasso had seen exhibitions of Iberian sculptures. From then on, he began trying out sculpture in a style that was inspired by them. His 1907 visit to an African tribal art exhibit in the Ethnological Museum in Paris also had a big impact on this work.

▼ *This African mask is an example of the so-called "primitive" art that had impressed Picasso.*

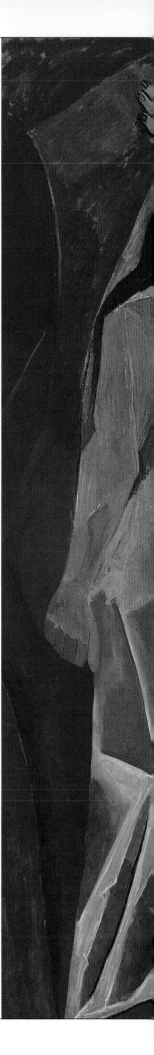

Cubism

Picasso had been struggling to find a way to show four dimensions on two-dimensional surfaces. It all started when he broke the rules with *Les Demoiselles d'Avignon*. To tackle this problem, Picasso, along with Georges Braque, developed a new language of painting called Cubism. Although most of the early works were landscapes and still lifes, Cubism was soon applied to portraiture as well.

The Principles of Perspective

Renaissance artists in the fifteenth century worked out a method called perspective to create the illusion of depth and distance on a flat picture surface. With an established viewpoint, objects are depicted smaller in proportion to how far back they are. Parallel lines reaching far back in space appear to get closer together and meet at the vanishing point. Artists who chose to depict realistic scenes used perspective.

▼ *These boxes have been drawn in perspective from three different angles. The distant sides appear smaller than the sides closest to us.*

Cubism, a New Perspective

In inventing Cubism, Picasso and Braque challenged the principles of perspective. By painting from several angles at once, they could show parts of the objects that could not otherwise be seen, an idea that Cézanne had started. Everything they depicted was broken down into geometric shapes. When a critic said that these paintings looked like "little cubes," the name Cubism stuck.

◀ Brick Factory in Tortosa *(1909), an early Cubist landscape.*

▶ *Detail of* Still Life of Apples and Pears in a Fruit Bowl *(1909). Still life was important for Cubism because artists could study the objects from different angles for as long as they wanted.*

▼ *This painting,* L'Estaque *(1906) by Braque, helped to give Picasso ideas for his own cubist landscape paintings.*

▼ *A detail of* The Sleeping Gypsy *(1897) by Rousseau. Rousseau described the delicate moonlight that illuminates these figures as "poetic."*

Henri Rousseau

People once laughed at the childlike pictures of Henri Rousseau, but nowadays his work is admired for its "naïve" or "primitive" style and the way he used his imagination. In 1908, Picasso bought one of Rousseau's paintings and organized a banquet — half serious, half mocking — in Rousseau's honor.

Friendship with Georges Braque

Picasso and Braque inspired each other with new ideas and exchanged ideas every day. Braque described their painting experiments as being like "two mountain-climbers roped together." Many works they created are so similar they cannot be distinguished from each other.

Art Dealers — Vollard and Kahnweiler

In 1901, the art dealer Ambroise Vollard (1865–1939) put on Picasso's first solo exhibition in Paris. Vollard bought nearly all Picasso's Rose Period paintings, but he refused to buy *Les Demoiselles d'Avignon*. However, in 1906, Picasso met another dealer, Daniel-Henry Kahnweiler (1884–1979), who bought all the sketches for *Les Demoiselles d'Avignon*. He would have bought the painting itself, but he could not afford it. Kahnweiler became Picasso's exclusive dealer.

▶ *Portrait of Ambroise Vollard (1910). Vollard was one of Picasso's most important supporters. His gallery in Paris, which opened in 1893, exhibited works by Cézanne, Picasso, and Matisse.*

Cubism and Collage

1912 Picasso's work is exhibited in Berliner Secession.
1912 His work is shown in Blaue Reiter exhibition in Munich, Germany.
1913 He returns to Barcelona for the funeral of his father. Apollinaire's *Cubist Painters* is published. It defines the principles of Cubism.
1914 Kahnweiler publishes a play by Max Jacob with illustrations by Picasso. World War I begins.

Picasso and Braque pushed Cubism into new stages. In 1912, Braque created textured surfaces by mixing paint with sand or plaster. Picasso also began adding objects such as newspapers and cardboard to his work. At this time, thanks to Kahnweiler, Picasso's work was popular in Germany. Meanwhile, for years, tension had been growing in Europe. At the outbreak of World War I in 1914, Picasso was torn between his German supporters and his chosen homeland of France.

Cubist Sculpture

Picasso explored cubist ideas in sculpture, too. In 1912, he created a sculpture of a guitar using sheet metal and wire. He emphasized geometric forms, distorted proportions, and recomposed the guitar by assembling different parts of the object in a new way.

◀ Guitar *(1912). This is one of the many images of guitars that Picasso made throughout his life. When a critic asked him, "What is it?" Picasso replied, "I call it a guitar."*

Dada

Some artists and writers gave birth to a movement against the social and cultural establishment. They produced several art objects and events that mocked the traditional ideas of art and literature. They claimed their art had no meaning at all. Even the name of the movement, Dada, is a nonsense word.

▶ *A 1917 "noise poem" by Hugo Ball. The words make no sense! Most Dada creations were supposed to be meaningless.*

KARAWANE
jolifanto bambla ô falli bambla
grossiga m'pfa habla horem
égiga goramen
higo bloiko russula huju
hollaka hollala
anlogo bung
blago bung
blago bung
bosso fataka
ü üü ü
schampa wulla wussa ólobo
hej tatta gôrem
eschige zunbada
ꟽulubu ssubudu uluꟽ ssubudu
tumba ba - umf
kusagauma
ba - umf
(1917)
Hugo Ball

Collage

By 1912, Picasso and Braque worked in collage, sticking all sorts of materials, such as newspapers, wallpaper, and music scores, onto their picture surfaces. Then they drew or painted over parts of these, often in bright colors. Sometimes the objects were used for their textures; in other instances, they were relevant to the picture's meaning.

▶ *Still Life with Chair Caning (1912) was Picasso's first collage. He painted the chair caning first and then framed it with rope to look like a gilded frame.*

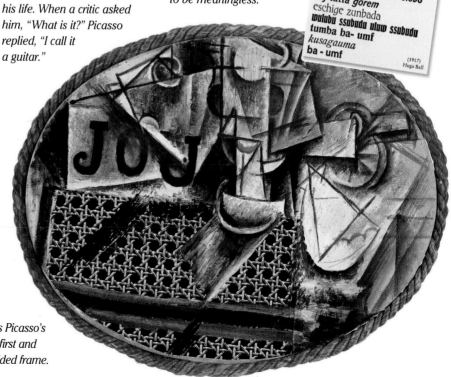

World War I

The appalling atrocities of World War I shattered everyone. Civilian lives were threatened as towns and villages were destroyed. The war also had a devastating impact for Picasso and his fellow artists. Although Picasso did not have to fight because he was Spanish, his French friends Braque, Derain, and Apollinaire were drafted into service. Because Picasso's dealer was German, his gallery was closed, and he had to flee the country.

◀ *During the horrors of World War I, millions were killed or injured.*

Eva

Before Fernande left Picasso, he was introduced to Marcelle Humbert (1885–1915). Picasso fell in love with her and called her Eva. Picasso never painted her portrait, but he referred to her in his works by including the words "ma jolie" (my pretty one) in them. They lived together in Paris and traveled in the South of France, but by 1915, Eva had become very ill and was hospitalized.

◀ *This photo of Eva with her dog was taken in 1912.*

Developments in Cubism

During the period from 1907–12, Picasso and Braque analyzed and represented objects from several viewpoints at once using subdued colors. This approach became known as Analytical Cubism. From 1912–14, their collages showed objects in their most broken-down forms, and stronger, brighter colors were used. This second phase of Cubism became known as Synthetic Cubism. Braque's style, however, began to go off in a different direction after the war, and the two artists never worked together again.

▶ Violin and Guitar *(1913) is an example of Picasso's Synthetic Cubist phase. Distorted parts of the instruments are recognizable, and pieces of wallpaper and colored paper make this picture more "real" than a traditional painting.*

High Society

▼ *A poster advertising the Ballets Russes.*

In 1916 Picasso's friend, the poet and playwright Jean Cocteau (1889–1963), introduced him to Sergey Diaghilev, founder of the famous Russian Ballet. Cocteau and Diaghilev were putting on a new ballet called *Parade*, and they asked Picasso to design the costumes and stage sets. The following year, Picasso met a dancer, Olga Kokhlova (1891–1955), and the world of ballet opened up a new phase in his career.

The Russian Ballet

At the beginning of the twentieth century, the Ballets Russes (Russian Ballet) led a revolution in dance. When Sergey Diaghilev (1872–1929) brought the ballet to Paris in 1909, enthusiasm was enormous. The theatrical gazette spoke of nothing else, while Parisians besieged the Théâtre du Chatelet for tickets. In 1912, the ballet's choreographer, Vaslav Nijinsky (1890–1950), created a sensation with his production of Debussy's *Prélude à l'après-midi d'un faune*.

Olga Kokhlova

Picasso met and fell in love with Olga, a ballerina with the Ballets Russes, in 1917 while he was designing for the ballet. They married in July 1918, and Picasso traveled with her and the Ballets Russes to Rome, Pompeii, Naples, Barcelona, and London, where he saw a great deal of Europe's artistic heritage. Back in Paris, they moved into a grand new apartment, and Olga introduced him to the "high society" of Paris.

◄ Portrait of Olga in an Armchair *(1917). Picasso painted this unfinished portrait of Olga when he first met her.*

Life in Paris

Although World War I had caused great dismay in France, Paris became dominant in art and culture once more. Picasso and Olga had a glittering social life, and he met important people, such as the Russian composer Igor Stravinsky (1882–1971). Olga banished all Picasso's art from their apartment, so he rented another apartment on the next floor and turned it into a studio and store.

► *Sketch of set for* Parade *(1917). When Picasso designed costumes and sets, some critics said that no serious artist would design for a ballet; others were impressed by his creativity.*

◀ *A light pole from the opulent Paris Opera House. In 1920, the ballet* Pulcinella, *composed by Stravinsky, premiered at the Opera House. Picasso designed the costumes and the set.*

Parade

The ballet *Parade* was based on an imaginary circus. It was first put on at the Théâtre du Chatelet in Paris in 1917. Picasso demonstrated a fresh burst of creativity when he designed the costumes and sets for it, taking ideas both from reality and from his imagination.

◀ *The composer Stravinsky was as revolutionary in his music as Picasso was in his art.*

▶ *This Chinese juggler was one of the costume designs by Picasso for* Parade.

Neoclassical Style

1921 Picasso's son Paulo is born. Author Maurice Raynal publishes the first monograph on his work. Picasso designs the curtains, sets, and costumes for the ballet *Cuadro Flamenco*.
1922 He spends the summer in Dinard, on France's northwest coast, with Olga and Paulo.
1923 Picasso's first major interview is published in English in a New York magazine. He etches a portrait of the author André Breton (1896–1966) for the title page of Breton's book, *Claire de Terre*.
1924 A collector buys *Les Demoiselles d'Avignon*.

Although Picasso created classical-type figure paintings while working with the ballet, he continued to paint some Cubist works, at times alternating between more conventional and abstract representation. During the early 1920s, Picasso's Neoclassical period began. He created his own kind of classical figures by borrowing elements from ancient art and combining them with his own sense of proportion, giving form to monumental and statuesque figures.

The Birth of Paulo

Picasso was almost forty when his son Paulo was born. Paulo was a new source of inspiration. Picasso spent hours watching him play and painted him often. Picasso also explored the close bond between mothers and children, painting many pictures on that theme.

▲ Woman and Child on the Seashore *(1921). Picasso, Olga, and Paulo spent the summers on the shores of the French Riviera, where Picasso created large-scale canvases depicting monumental classical-type figures.*

Changing Styles

In the summer of 1921, Picasso painted two versions of the huge canvas *Three Musicians*. It was the first time he had used a group of people as a cubist subject. The figures were Pulcinella, Harlequin, and a monk, stock characters from Italian theater. Each character was broken down into geometric shapes and reassembled. Many art critics saw the painting, with its sharp color and contrast of light and shadow, as the climax of Synthetic Cubism.

◀ Three Musicians *(1921). Some say that the figure of Pulcinella represents Apollinaire, the monk represents Max Jacob, and the figure of Harlequin represents Picasso himself.*

Classical Figures

Picasso also borrowed ideas from archaic and early Renaissance art. His powerful-looking figures, made up of exaggerated proportions and simplified forms, are a result of all these ideas. Using contrasting tones, he made his figures look three-dimensional, almost like classical statues, reminding viewers of ancient art.

▶ The Pipes of Pan *(1923) was painted from over fifty studies. It was seen as the most important painting of this period.*

Classical Theater

Picasso continued working with the Ballets Russes on sets for *Le Tricorne* and *Pulcinella*. In 1922, Cocteau asked Picasso to design the sets for his reworking of *Antigone*, a play by the ancient Greek writer Sophocles. Just two days before the play began, Picasso produced the finished set made of chalk on a huge sheet of crumpled canvas. Inspired by classical themes, it was a magnificent success.

▲ *This ancient Greek mask shows a tragic character. Masks were worn in plays like* Antigone *to portray characters' emotions. The actors changed masks to show different emotions.*

▶ The Grand Odalisque *(1814) by Ingres was admired for the way it was painted with smooth, gleaming skin tones, similar to Renaissance art.*

Neoclassical style

Picasso had long admired the work of the painter Jean-Auguste-Dominique Ingres (1780–1867), leader of the nineteenth-century French neoclassical school of painting. Picasso's vast figure paintings of this period show his interest in Ingres' style.

Dinard and Surrealism

By 1924, Picasso was extremely successful. He became interested in the new ideas developed by the Surrealist movement. Although Picasso never became an official member of the movement, his art gained new dimensions. Many people called this his Monster period because his art was characterized by fantastic and grotesque images.

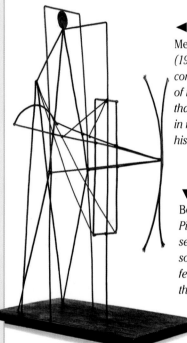

◀ *Maquette for a Memorial to Apollinaire (1928). This wire construction was one of the small sculptures that Picasso designed in remembrance of his friend.*

▼ *Bathers on the Beach (1928) is from Picasso's Dinard series. There are some simple facial features, even though the shapes look as if they are made of stone.*

Wire Sculpture

In the Paris studio of Spanish sculptor Julio González (1876–1942), Picasso made four wire and metal constructions. He offered two of these as designs for a monument to his friend Apollinaire, who had died at the end of World War I, but they were turned down.

The Bathers of Dinard

During the summer of 1928, Picasso took Olga and Paulo to Dinard in Brittany in northwest France. There, Picasso produced a series of paintings of bathers, but unlike his neoclassical figures, these were distorted and deformed. Some were rounded and curved, and others were jagged. These paintings became known as his Dinard series and were also part of his Monster period.

Marie-Thérèse Walter

The fashionable world that Olga created for Picasso began to stifle him. In 1927, he met seventeen-year-old Marie-Thérèse Walter (1909–77), and although she was less than half his age, he fell in love. He was inspired with a new wave of creativity, and Marie-Thérèse became the subject of a whole series of works.

◀ The Red Armchair *(c. 1929). Picasso shows both the face and profile of his sitter in this portrait of Marie-Thérèse.*

▼ The Persistence of Memory *(1931) by Salvador Dalí is one of the most famous Surrealist paintings. A strange, fleshy shape lies on the sand, and metal clocks are soft and floppy: time is at an end. It is like a weird dream.*

Surrealism

The Surrealist movement, which originated in French literature, sought to fuse the dream world and reality. Like Dada, it was a reaction against rationalism, but it expressed a more positive spirit. In 1924, Picasso knew many of the most important Surrealists, including Giorgio de Chirico (1888–1978), Man Ray (1890–1976), and fellow Spanish artist Salvador Dalí (1904–89).

◀ *This photo of the founders of the Surrealist movement — André Breton, Paul Éluard (1895–1952), Tristan Tzara (1896–1963), and Benjamin Péret (1899–1959) — was taken in 1920.*

▶ *Sigmund Freud, the doctor who decoded dreams and gave the Surrealists their starting point.*

Sigmund Freud

The psychiatrist Sigmund Freud (1856–1939) discovered that our subconscious minds are extremely powerful. In his *The Interpretation of Dreams* (1899), he explored and analyzed the subconscious, examining the complex and symbolic world of dreams. As the founder of psychoanalysis, his theories inspired Surrealism and paved the way for modern psychology and psychiatry.

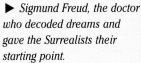

The Minotaur

1932 Picasso selects 238 works for a show in Paris.
1933 He produces a large number of graphic works with the Minotaur as the subject, including *Vollard Suite* and the cover for the first issue of *Minotaure* magazine. Fernande Olivier publishes her memoirs, and Picasso tries to ban sales of the book for fear of Olga's jealousy.
1934 He visits Spain, and after his return to Paris, he produces many drawings and paintings of bullfights.
1935 He produces some etchings called *Minotauromachy* and begins to write and illustrate surrealist poetry. When Marie-Thérèse becomes pregnant, Olga leaves him. His daughter Maya is born. Jaime Sabartés moves to Paris and becomes his secretary.
1936 He meets Dora Maar. The Spanish Civil War begins. He is appointed honorary director of the Prado Museum in Madrid.

In the early 1930s, Picasso had more contact with the Surrealists and became fascinated with the classical myth of the Minotaur. The Minotaur, with the head of a bull and body of a man, appeared in many of Picasso's works. The Minotaur represented several things, such as Picasso himself and the rise of violence in the world.

▼ *Detail of Picasso's design for the magazine cover* Minotaure *(1933). He drew the Minotaur in pencil and then stuck it on top of a collage of cardboard, ribbon, doilies, wallpaper, and leaves.*

Minotaure

Picasso painted the Minotaur at the same time as the rise of Nazism — a political party led by Adolf Hitler (1889–1945) — in Germany. The Surrealists also took up the Minotaur as a symbol of social concern. Then in 1933, a Surrealist magazine called *Minotaure* was launched. When Olga left Picasso in 1935, he became depressed and could not paint for months. In the end, he created an etching showing his troubled state. Called *Minotauromachy*, it shows a Minotaur invading a sculptor's studio.

▶ *The Crucifixion after Grünewald (1932). Picasso used black ink, not paint, and kept the background dark.*

▼ *The Crucifixion (c .1510-15) by Grünewald is a powerful image of suffering and grief in a deserted, ghostly landscape. Christ's body on the cross is twisted and bleeding. The mourners are overcome.*

The Crucifixion

Throughout his career, Picasso produced his own versions of many old master works. In 1932, he produced a series of works on the Christian motif of the crucifixion, inspired by the German Renaissance artist Matthias Grünewald (c. 1480–1528). In Picasso's version, shapes represent the figures from the original painting. By creating these shapes, Picasso shows the emotions of the figures rather than their physical features.

▲ Bullfight: Death of the Toreador *(1933). One of Picasso's first pictures had been of a bullfight. This painting is contorted and colorful and shows confusion, fear, and pain.*

The Bullfight

Picasso attended bullfights as a young boy with his father in Spain, and his interest in the bullfight never waned. The bull, found in many of his works, became an important symbol in Picasso's art.

The *Vollard Suite*

The *Vollard Suite* is a series of one hundred engravings that Picasso dedicated to his old friend, the art dealer Ambroise Vollard. Picasso created ninety-seven of them first, on four themes — The Battle of Love, The Sculptor's Studio, Rembrandt, and The Minotaur. Picasso felt particularly passionate about these themes at the time. In 1937, he produced three portraits of Vollard to complete the series.

◀ *This etching from the* Vollard Suite *(1933) shows the Minotaur asleep while a young woman, Marie-Thérèse, sits and watches him.*

1937 Picasso works on many portraits of both Dora Maar and Marie-Thérèse. Maar finds a studio in Paris large enough for him to work on the *Guernica* mural. In June, *Guernica* is completed and installed inside the entrance to the Spanish Pavilion at the World's Fair. He continues to make drawings and etchings on themes and subjects of *Guernica*. He spends part of the summer with Maar in Mougins, in southeast France, where he paints a variety of subjects. He travels to Switzerland and visits his sick friend, artist Paul Klee (1879–1940). The Museum of Modern Art in New York buys *Les Demoiselles d'Avignon*.

Guernica

In 1937, even though Spain was in the midst of the Civil War, the Republican government asked Picasso to create a mural for Spain's pavilion at the Paris World's Fair. Then on April 26, when news broke of a bombing raid by the German air force on a defenseless Spanish town called Guernica, Picasso was inspired. He painted *Guernica* to show the horror of the event, using only shades of black and white and bullfight imagery to represent violence and bloodshed.

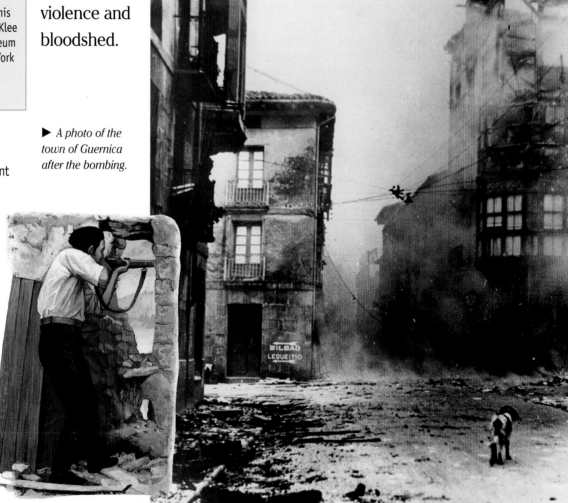

▶ *A photo of the town of Guernica after the bombing.*

Spain at War

Since 1931, Spain had been undergoing violent social and political upheaval. In July 1936, the Spanish Civil War began when the Spanish army rebelled against the elected Republican government. General Francisco Franco (1892– 1975) led the army with the help of Italy and Germany.

▶ *An armed Republican fighter during the Civil War.*

Dora Maar

In 1936, Picasso met Dora Maar (1907–97), a surrealist artist and photographer. She photographed *Guernica* as Picasso worked on it. The photos were later published in a magazine. Although he remained involved with Marie-Thérèse, Dora became Picasso's companion. He painted several portraits of Dora and also paintings showing grief, using lines and color to emphasize the idea of distress.

▶ The Weeping Woman *(1937) is another painting about the horrors of Guernica. Using Dora Maar as a model, Picasso painted sharp Cubist angles. The woman is biting on her handkerchief, which turns to ice as she watches her town being destroyed. She is wearing her best Sunday hat, and the bombers are reflected in her eyes.*

Guernica

The Spanish Government

When the Spanish general Franco overthrew the Republican government, he became the head of Spain until his death in 1975. Although he had visions of restoring Spanish grandeur after the Civil War, he was never popular because he was a dictator. Despite his many years in France, Picasso was still Spanish and fervently opposed to Franco. Besides painting *Guernica* and *The Weeping Woman*, he wrote a poem and made two etchings called *The Dream and Lie of Franco* as a form of protest.

◀ *General Franco, who became Spain's absolute ruler for nearly forty years.*

▼ Guernica *(1937) shows the terrors of war. The bull symbolizes brutality and evil, the wounded horse represents the Spanish people, and the light bulb refers to the explosion of the bomb over the town. In the pyramidlike composition, dying and desperate figures are distorted with grief and pain. A woman carries a dead baby, another woman falls through a burning building, and a dead soldier holds a broken sword.*

Preparatory Drawings

Picasso began working on *Guernica* on May first, and by mid-June, the mural was installed in the pavilion. He made forty-five sketches and studies before he started on the actual painting, experimenting with parts and changing the composition several times.

▶ Study of a Horse *(1937). Picasso drew several horses before deciding on the final one. It represents the brave and defenseless people of Guernica.*

The World at War

Unlike many artists, Picasso stayed in Paris during the German occupation. Some of his works from this time show the gloominess of the war years, while other works are lighthearted and amusing. He also began making sculpture from objects he found lying around. *Head of a Bull* was made from an ordinary bicycle seat and handlebars.

Maya

Although, after 1938, Picasso drifted apart from Marie-Thérèse, he continued to visit their daughter Maya. He painted numerous portraits of Maya with her toys in a childlike style, perhaps trying to ignore the war around him.

► Portrait of Maya with her Doll *(1938).* *Untroubled by the world, the little girl with large purple eyes is holding her doll. Picasso's portraits of Maya are based on the innocence of children's paintings.*

Occupied Paris

In September 1939, Britain and France declared war on Germany after Germany invaded Poland. The Germans swept through Belgium and Luxembourg and invaded France in May 1940. Many people in France wanted to put up a fight, but millions of French men had been killed in World War I, and many French people did not support a war effort. Paris surrendered on June 14, and the Germans occupied France. Many of Picasso's friends who were in hiding had been arrested or forced into exile. The Nazis enforced restrictions, but they offered Picasso special treatment, which he refused to accept. He was not afraid to show his contempt. One day, when a German officer saw a photo of *Guernica,* he asked Picasso, "Did you do this?" Picasso replied, "No, you did."

◄ *German troops entering Paris on June 14, 1940. They occupied the city until 1944.*

Royan

At the beginning of the war, Picasso stayed in Royan on the Atlantic coast near Bordeaux. He moved there with Sabartés, Marie-Thérèse, Maya, and Dora. Occasionally he traveled back and forth between Royan and Paris, but it was not easy with the German occupation. His unsettled life made it difficult for him to paint large-scale canvases, so he filled many sketchbooks with pencil drawings. By the end of August 1940, he returned to Paris and remained there.

▲ Café at Royan (1940) is one of the few paintings that Picasso did during this period.

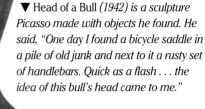

▼ Head of a Bull (1942) is a sculpture Picasso made with objects he found. He said, "One day I found a bicycle saddle in a pile of old junk and next to it a rusty set of handlebars. Quick as a flash . . . the idea of this bull's head came to me."

Jaime Sabartés

By the end of 1935, the Spanish poet Jaime Sabartés, Picasso's old friend, was working as his secretary. They had become quite close and lived together or near each other until the end of the war. Picasso depicted Sabartés in many of his works from the time they met in Barcelona in 1899.

▶ Portrait of Jaime Sabartés as a Spanish Grandee (1939) was painted in Royan.

After the War

1944 Jacob dies in a German concentration camp. A private reading of Picasso's play *Le Désir Attrapé par la Queue* is directed by the author-playwright Albert Camus (1913–1960).

1945 World War II ends. Picasso begins working with lithography (printing). A Picasso and Matisse joint exhibit is held at the Victoria and Albert Museum, London.

1946 He paints many portraits of Françoise, now his new love. He takes her to Nice to meet Matisse. Gertrude Stein dies.

1947 Picasso gives ten pictures to the National Museum of Modern Art in Paris. Françoise gives birth to their son Claude.

1948 Picasso, Françoise, and Claude move to a villa in Vallauris on the French Riviera, where he makes ceramics. He attends a peace conference in Wroclaw.

In 1944, Paris was freed from occupation. On hearing about the Nazi concentration camps that came to light after the war, Picasso began painting a tribute to the victims of the Holocaust. Although he never finished the painting, *The Charnel House* portrays the brutality of the war's aftermath. Picasso painted horribly distorted, broken bodies in shades of black and white in a way similar to *Guernica*.

▶ The Bull *(1945) is one of a series of eleven lithographs of bulls that Picasso made. This one shows different angles like a cubist image.*

Lithography

In 1945, Braque introduced Picasso to Fernand Mourlot (1895–1988), a lithographer who showed Picasso the technique of making lithographs. Working in Mourlot's studio, Picasso became fascinated with the technique and went on to produce over two hundred lithographs during his career.

LIBERATION

In a 1944 operation known as D-Day, Allied troops invaded France to drive out German forces. Although many lives were lost, the operation brought an end to German occupation.

◀ *Allied soldiers from Britain, France, Australia, and the United States came to liberate France from German occupation in 1944.*

Picasso at the Salon

The official annual exhibition of the Salon d'Automne of 1944 was called *Salon de la Libération*. The exhibit included seventy-four paintings and five sculptures by Picasso. It was the first time Picasso's works were on display at the Salon, and problems arose. The day before the exhibition opened, the news broke that Picasso had joined the French Communist Party, and several people who were against the Communists tried to tear his paintings off the walls.

◀ *A poster of the French Communist Party.*

Pottery

In 1946, Picasso visited the annual potters exhibition in Vallauris on the French Riviera, where pottery had been made since antiquity. The following summer, Picasso returned and was welcomed into the Madoura workshop, where he learned the technique. In just one year, he created two thousand pieces. His plates, jugs, and vases were fanciful and amusing, and they offered Picasso yet another medium in which to juggle decoration and form.

◄ Woman with a Mantilla *(1949), one of Picasso's pottery creations.*

▼ The Charnel House *(1944–45). Some scholars believe that Picasso was inspired by images of concentration camps appearing in the news during the time.*

▲ *Picasso in his workshop studio in Antibes.*

Antibes

In 1945, Picasso stayed in Antibes in the South of France with Dora. While he was there, the town council asked him to decorate the inside of the town's castle, which was used as a cultural center. Over the next two years, he returned with Françoise. He was given some studios to work in and developed his White Period.

War and Peace

1949 Françoise gives birth to their daughter Paloma. Picasso buys an old factory in Vallauris and turns it into a sculpture studio.
1950 Picasso is made an honorary citizen of Vallauris. The Korean War begins when Communist forces from North Korea invade South Korea. Millions are killed.
1951 *Massacre in Korea* is exhibited in Paris. Picasso visits Matisse, who is ill.
1952 He completes his second play, *Les Quatres Petites Filles*.
1953 Françoise leaves Picasso and moves to Paris with the children. Picasso meets Jacqueline Roque (1926–86). Sabartés gives his collection of Picasso paintings to the city of Barcelona.

After joining the Communist Party in 1944, Picasso became involved with the Peace Movement. In 1949, the Paris World Peace Conference adopted the dove that he had designed as their symbol of peace. Picasso used his fame to stand up for human rights and protested against various conflicts. In 1950 and again in 1962, he was awarded the Lenin Peace Prize. When his companion Françoise Gilot gave birth to their second child, they named her Paloma, which means "dove" in Spanish.

Family Life
Picasso had two homes with Françoise and their two children Claude and Paloma, one in Paris and the other in the hills above Vallauris. He was inspired by his children, and he created many portraits of them. He also taught the children to paint and swim. Photographers and tourists often came to the beach to catch a glimpse of him.

► *Picasso with Françoise, Claude, and Paloma.*

▼ Peace *(1952). This mural for the chapel in Vallauris shows total happiness: mothers relax, and children play around Pegasus, the flying horse.*

Sculpture: New Material

Picasso began to collect objects he found around Vallauris and make them into sculptures, or *assemblages*. He used plaster to bind the bits and pieces that he found lying around, and then he cast the whole thing in bronze. He had started this idea of making sculptures from objects he found during the war. (See *Head of a Bull* on page 37.)

Art for Peace

After living through so many dark war years, Picasso was passionate about peace. When his dove was used on the poster for the World Peace Congress, it became world famous. Picasso continued to create works to focus attention on political concerns. In 1951, he painted *Massacre in Korea* in protest of the American invasion of North Korea.

▼ *Picasso made* Goat *(1950) out of a wicker basket, flowerpots, palm leaves, china, cardboard, metal, and plaster.*

▲ The Dove *(1949). This Christian symbol of the Holy Spirit also became the symbol of peace. It was used on stamps and many antiwar posters.*

The Chapel in Vallauris

Picasso's art was not only a political statement but also expressed his humanitarian interests. In 1952, he designed two huge murals for a fourteenth-century deconsecrated chapel in Vallauris. In the light of the war that was raging in Korea at the time, he decided to make it a temple of peace, drawing over 250 sketches for the two murals — one on peace and the other on war. The completed murals were installed in 1954.

▼ War *(1952), representing violence and conflict, shows a chariot of death being driven toward a huge figure holding the symbols of justice and peace.*

The Artist at Work

By now, Picasso's work was known around the world. In 1953, he had met Jacqueline Roque, and by 1954, when his relationship with Françoise was completely over, she became his love and his muse, inspiring much of his late work. He painted himself painting his model over and again. Picasso and Jacqueline left Paris and moved to a nineteenth-century villa on a hilltop overlooking Cannes, where the Mediterranean made him happy, reminding him of Barcelona.

Les Ménines

In 1957, Picasso began to paint a series of works based on the 1656 masterpiece by Velázquez, *Las Meninas*, a work he had admired during a visit to the Prado Museum in Madrid. He was particularly interested in the subject of artist and model that was featured in *Las Meninas*. When the studio on the lower level of his villa La Californie became too distracting, he moved to the top floor. He worked for several months, producing over forty works on this theme.

▶ *Picasso's* Les Ménines *(1957) has a composition similar to Velázquez's painting but is painted in his broken, distorted style.*

▼ *Velázquez's* Las Meninas *(1656) shows the Spanish princess, her servants, and Velázquez himself, standing at his easel and working on a huge painting of them.*

The Artist and Model Series

In 1963, Picasso began working on a large number of works on the subject of the artist and his model. Scholars have argued that the model in these works is not considered as an actual person but simply represents a part of reality. Therefore, the artist's perception and depiction of that reality becomes the true subject of these pieces.

◀ The Painter and his Model *(1963). This is one of many works in the series.*

La Californie: Remembering Matisse

Picasso and Matisse had developed a lifelong friendship, and Matisse's death had left Picasso grief stricken. As a tribute to his friend, Picasso painted his studio at La Californie in a style similar to Matisse's style. The work, which can be considered a painting within a painting, is more than just a picture of his studio. Metaphorically, the studio is a portrait of Picasso's own creative process.

◀ Portrait of Jacqueline *(1957). Picasso produced many portraits of Jacqueline, trying out new styles.*

▲ *A photo of Picasso with Jacqueline. He met her in a pottery shop in Vallauris.*

At Home with Jacqueline

From 1958, Picasso moved back and forth between La Californie and his new residence, the Château of Vauvenargues. It was large enough to house his huge art collection, and he lived there happily with Jacqueline. He continued doing what he always had — producing art. Toward the end of Picasso's life, the media had turned him into a celebrity, taking away his privacy by wanting to know everything about him. He stayed at home more often to hide from the press and the public's prying eyes.

▶ The Studio at La Californie *(1956). Ironically, a blank white canvas is the focal point of this work.*

An Accomplished Artist

Observing a group of children, Picasso said: "When I was as old as these children, I could draw like Raphael, but it took me a lifetime to learn to draw like them." Although he was able to create works in the classical tradition like the old masters, Picasso wanted to depict reality as it is seen through the eyes of a child. During the last years of his life, he drew and painted with amazing energy. His late works continued to show his determination not to fit into categories.

Nesjar and New Sculpture

Picasso met a Norwegian sculptor named Carl Nesjar (born 1920) who worked in sheet metal and concrete. In 1957, Nesjar introduced Picasso to his own technique for sculpting concrete by sandblasting. Nesjar later made huge concrete reliefs based on Picasso's designs.

The Artist

Living in Cannes was becoming increasingly difficult for Picasso. In 1961, after their wedding, Picasso and Jacqueline moved to an isolated villa located on a hill near Mougins, about five miles away from Cannes, to escape from the crowds. He spent the rest of his life working in this new residence, Notre-Dame-de-Vie. In his last years, he worked on many self-portraits. As with most of his later works, they are drawn and painted in simple, childlike styles. Like his *Portrait of Maya with her Doll* (page 36), the main features are the eyes.

▲ Football Player *(1961) was made from sheet metal by Picasso and Nesjar. The enormous, flat footballer is about to kick a ball. His waving outlines make him appear full of energy. Picasso loved making his work huge.*

◀ *This self-portrait,* Seated Man *(1965), was painted in Mougins. Picasso depicted himself wearing his favorite striped T-shirt.*

◀ The Louvre museum, Paris. A unique exhibition was held here to mark Picasso's ninetieth birthday.

Picasso's Birthday Celebrations

On his seventieth and eightieth birthdays, many celebrations were held in Picasso's honor. For his eightieth birthday, an exhibition was put up at the Museum of Modern Art in New York. On his ninetieth birthday, President Pompidou opened an exhibition at the Louvre, an honor never before paid to a living artist. Many other special exhibitions were held throughout the world.

▶ Picasso's large-scale sculpture Head of a Woman, *standing 50 feet (over 15 meters) high, was erected in 1967.*

◀Picasso appeared on the cover of The Sunday Times Magazine *in 1965.*

Monumental Sculpture

In 1964, Picasso was asked by an American architectural firm to design a monumental sculpture for the Civic Center Plaza in Chicago. By 1965, Picasso completed the model for *Head of a Woman*, and construction of the full-scale steel sculpture was soon underway. Although the abstract figure was surrounded by controversy when it was unveiled, it soon became one of Chicago's most treasured landmarks. Picasso refused payment for his work and donated the design as well as the model to the city of Chicago and its people. Picasso never traveled to America and never got to see the realization of his project.

His Last Years

Picasso spent the last years of his life working, creating mainly drawings and graphic designs. Even his latest works, including drawings done between 1971 and 1972, were exhibited by galleries. In the winter of 1973, he caught influenza, which left him weak, but he resumed working in the spring. On April 8, he died, leaving behind a priceless inheritance.

◀Picasso was buried on April 10, 1973, on the grounds of his home, the Château of Vauvenargues.

Glossary

abstract A style of art that does not represent objects as they appear in reality but reduces and simplifies forms and objects. Abstract art abandons the traditional principle that art must imitate nature.

Analytical Cubism The first phase of Cubism, which lasted until 1912. It simplified forms into geometric shapes and used a limited range of colors.

Art Nouveau An ornamental style of European and U.S. art that lasted from 1890 to 1910, characterized by the use of long, curving lines based on plant forms. This so-called "new" style (the word nouveau means "new" in French) was applied primarily to architecture, interior design, jewelry, glass design, and illustration.

assemblages Components put together for a certain purpose; collections of things or groups of people.

avant-garde A term used to refer to persons or actions that are different or experimental, particularly with respect to the arts.

château A large country house or castle in France.

choreographer Someone who creates new dances.

classical Term used to describe works of art from ancient Greece or Rome, or works that have the same characteristics as the works of ancient Greece or Rome.

collage A picture made by sticking together bits of paper or other materials.

Communism A political system that favors a classless society and collective ownership of goods and services.

composition The arrangement of the parts of something. Term used to refer to the way in which objects are arranged, usually in a painting or sculpture.

Cubism An art movement of the early twentieth century that aimed to represent three dimensions on a two-dimensional plane. Cubist artists represented objects from more than one angle so that several different aspects of the subject could be seen at the time.

curator Someone who looks after the exhibits or documents in a museum or library.

Dadaism An anti-art movement started in 1915 that attempted to express the confusion and disorder of the world after World War I by rejecting traditional culture and ideas of beauty in art.

engraving The process of carving a design into a block of wood or plate of metal, or the prints taken from this process.

etching A method of engraving in which a design is burned onto a metal plate using acid, or the print taken from the process.

Futurism A politically-driven art movement that began in Italy in 1909. It glorified the modern world of machinery, speed, and violence.

Grandee A Spanish or Portuguese nobleman of high rank.

Holocaust The Nazi extermination of millions of Jews during World War II.

Impressionism A nineteenth-century art movement that took a more spontaneous approach to painting, attempting to capture and portray the atmosphere of a given moment, usually identified by a strong concern for the changing qualities of light.

linocut A print made from a design cut into a piece of linoleum.

lithography The process of printing by pressing paper onto a stone that has been engraved and treating it with chemicals and water.

muse A person who inspires an artist's work.

naïve Unsophisticated or simple.

Nazism The National Socialist regime of Hitler's Germany (1933 to 1945); the political beliefs and methods of Hilter's party.

Neoclassicism A European art movement of the late eighteenth and early nineteenth century that tried to re-create the classical style of ancient Greece and Rome.

Neoplasticism The term used by Piet Mondrian (1872–1944), who believed that art does not have to depict nature as it appears, to describe his style of abstract art characterized by simplistic compositions of straight lines and rectangles and the use of primary colors.

pavilion A large tent or canopy put up for a short period of time used for public exhibitions or shows.

perspective The method of representing objects so as to make them appear three-dimensional. The illusion of depth and space, or a view extending far into the distance.

Postimpressionism A term applied to a number of painters of the late nineteenth and early twentieth centuries whose style developed out of or reacted against that of the Impressionists.

primitive Simplistic or crude, tribal.

psychoanalysis The study and interpretation of unconscious thoughts and dreams.

Renaissance The cultural movement, originating in Italy during the fourteenth century and lasting until the seventeenth century, in which the art, literature, and ideas of ancient Greece were rediscovered and applied to the arts. The artistic style of this period.

Surrealism An aesthetic movement of the 1920s and 1930s that attempted to portray thought, dreams, and the imagination.

Synthetic Cubism The second or later phase of Cubism. It began after 1912 and used stronger colors and more complex forms and started to incorporate the use of collage.

Index

Index